ELEMENTARY/MIDDLE SCHOOL PERCUSSION ENSEMBLES

D.R.U.M.
DISCIPLINE, RESPECT, AND UNITY THROUGH MUSIC
By JIM SOLOMON

D.R.U.M. 1998 Osceola Elementary School

Editor: DEBBIE CAVALIER
Cover Illustrator: JOSEPH KLUCAR
Layout Design: THAIS YANES

© 1998 BELWIN-MILLS PUBLISHING CORP. (ASCAP)
All Rights Assigned to and Controlled by ALFRED MUSIC PUBLISHING CO., INC.
All Rights Reserved   Printed in U.S.A.

CONTENTS

D.R.U.M. MEMBERSHIP CERTIFICATE 3

INTRODUCTION 4
    Forming a Group 5
    D.R.U.M. CODE 5
    Using Drums in the Classroom 6
    Fostering the Creative 6
    The Power of a Strong Music Program 6

JAM RHYTHMS AND JAM RHYTHM ENSEMBLE 7
    Jam Rhythms 8
    Jam Rhythm Ensembles 8
    Customizing the Ensemble for Your Players 9
    Notation/Rote 9
    Difficulty Ratings 10
    Jam Rhythms in 4/4 11
    Jam Rhythm Ensembles in 4/4 14
    Jam Rhythms in 6/8 22
    Jam Rhythm Ensembles in 6/8 24
    Jam Rhythms in 3/4 27
    Jam Rhythm Ensembles in 3/4 29

ENSEMBLES BASED ON SPEECH 31
    MONKEY, MONKEY MOO 32
    PIGS LIKE MUD 33
    TINY SURFER 34
    ORDER IN THE GALLERY! 35
    PETER, PETER IF YOU'RE ABLE 36
    IF YOU SEE A MONKEY 37
    SODA POP 38
    OLD JOHN TUCKER 39
    DR. FELL 40
    RIQUE, RIQUE, RIQUE, RAN 41
    JACK BE NIMBLE 42
    AWAKE, ARISE 43

APPENDIX 44
    Form 45
    Improvisation 46
    Teaching Suggestions 47
    Building an Ensemble with Student-Created Rhythms 49
    Instrument Technique 50

D.R.U.M.

_____
Student's Name

D = **Discipline - People with self-discipline are stronger.**

R = **Respect - People with self-respect make good decisions. People who respect others make the world a better place.**

U = **Unity - We work together. Say, "we" not "I."**

M = **Music !!!**

INTRODUCTION

Kids love drums! The sight, the sound, the power, and the feel are tremendous motivators for many students. When played in ensemble, drums require the discipline of the participants to work together. The payoff is immediate: a dynamic, forceful, expressive sound that is greater than the sum of its parts. Whether it be with general music classes or with a special group, drum ensemble gives music teachers a powerful tool to build teamwork, discipline, and excitement in their students.

D.R.U.M. was formed at my elementary school in 1995 to provide an ensemble experience for some fifth grade students who were not involved in any of the regular music groups. For a variety of reasons they were not in the chorus, recorder club, or the Orff instrumental group.

D.R.U.M. is an acronym for Discipline, Respect, and Unity through Music. The importance of teamwork and self-discipline is stressed as the members learn intensive percussion ensembles. They are expected to keep up with their school work and show good behavior to stay in the group. The group blends students with different behavioral, academic, and social backgrounds. They play music from the United States, Brazil, Africa, and China.

Congas are used as the lead drums. The conga drum is an ideal instrument for creating and performing parts in percussion ensembles with upper elementary and middle school students. By using only *Bass* and *Tone* (open tone), students and teachers can achieve instant success and play rhythms with powerful tonal contrast.

Drums provide unlimited potential for experience in rhythm, ensemble, movement, improvisation, meter, and timbre—the musical learning can be extensive. Drum ensemble provides teachers with the flexibility to assign parts of varying difficulty to players of different abilities. Moreover, the ensembles provide an invaluable social experience because the players depend on each other for the group to succeed.

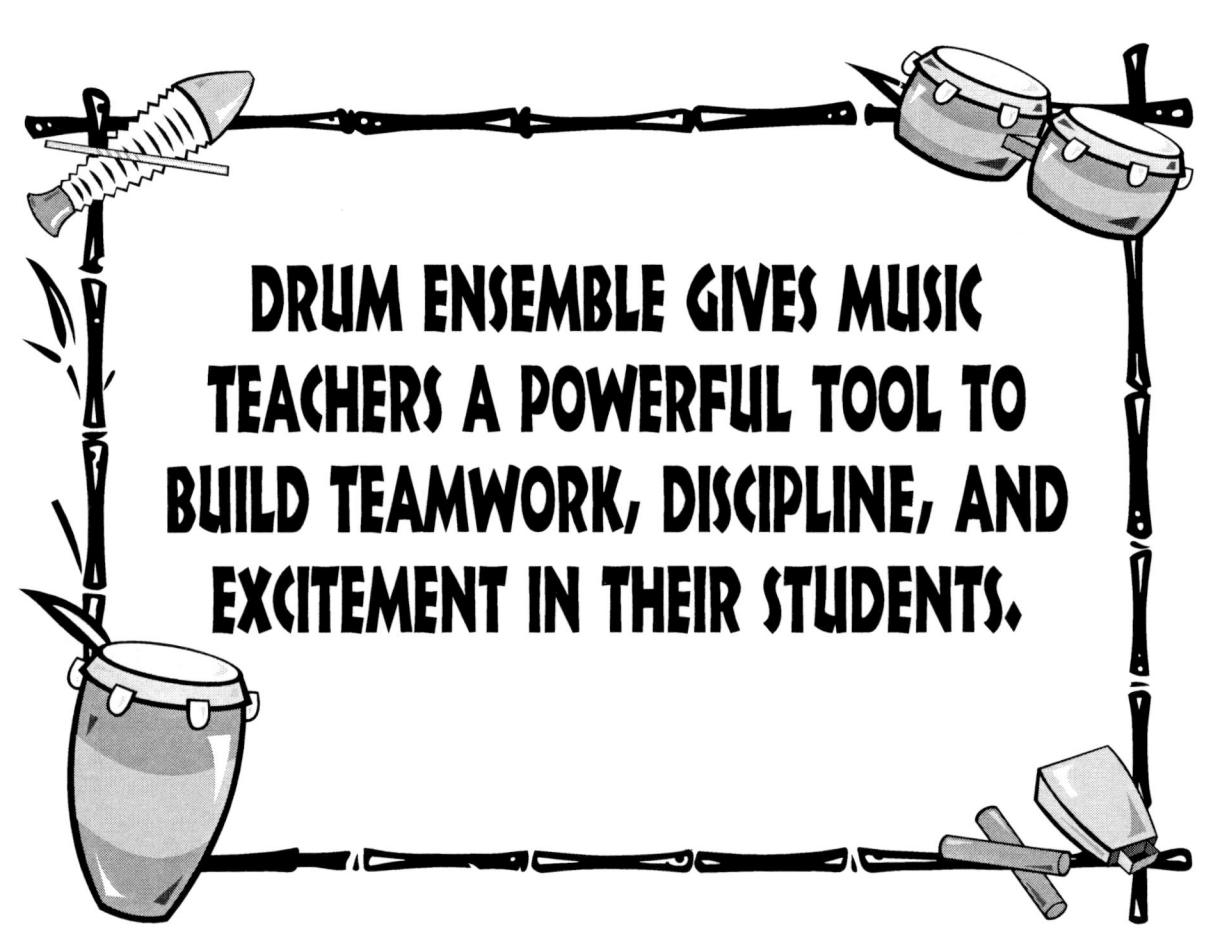

DRUM ENSEMBLE GIVES MUSIC TEACHERS A POWERFUL TOOL TO BUILD TEAMWORK, DISCIPLINE, AND EXCITEMENT IN THEIR STUDENTS.

FORMING A GROUP

The process of forming a percussion ensemble is unique to every teaching situation. At my school, students are "auditioned," but not in a formal audition situation. Rather, I take notes throughout the fourth and early fifth grade years on which students can play the different percussion and Orff instrument parts that we work on during general music class. This process helps me become familiar with the students who can play difficult parts in ensemble.

It's important to note that the skills required to play a conga, recorder, bass xylophone, or glockenspiel are somewhat different. A good glockenspiel player is not necessarily a good conga drummer. Students who can play the samba agogo bell pattern and drum patterns with sixteenth notes come under strong consideration for D.R.U.M.

After the "auditioning" process is complete, permission slips are sent home. Usually, the group is limited to fifth graders, but occasionally fourth graders are invited. Our group size varies from 12 to 18 students. We meet one hour a week after school or 20 minutes twice a week during school.

D.R.U.M. CODE

At our first meeting, members are given the "D.R.U.M. Code." (See page 3. The line under the word "D.R.U.M." is where each student's name is filled in when they receive their personal copy.) They are asked to take it home, study it, and put it in a special place. The meaning is discussed whenever needed at our rehearsals: for example, we examine how people with self-discipline really are stronger people, and that if they have self-respect they will make good decisions that will help them instead of create problems. If they show respect to others, others will like them. If they show unity in our group and work together, they will not be saying, "I want to play this, I want to do that," but they will be talking about what is best for the whole group's performance. Whenever a behavior situation arises in the group, we discuss it in reference to showing discipline, respect, and unity.

If a student is having significant behavior problems in other areas at school, the student, his/her teacher, and I have a three-way conference. We devise a plan. Noticeable effort towards improvement must follow. The student still attends rehearsals, but if the problem continues, he/she must work on the plan to improve the situation, write apology letters if necessary, finish important work if necessary, etc., instead of playing drums during the rehearsals. Usually the motivation to be in the group is so strong that this approach is successful.

The code is recited by our D.R.U.M. announcers at the beginning of each performance. All members of the group say the last line together before the tempo is counted off for our first piece.

The name of our group is D.R.U.M.

- **D** stands for Discipline. People with self-discipline are stronger.
- **R** stands for Respect. People with self-respect make good decisions.
  People who respect others make the world a better place.
- **U** stands for Unity. We work together. Say, "we" not "I."
- **M** stands for Music!

D.R.U.M. stands for Discipline, Respect, and Unity through Music!

We make this recitation a part of our announcements in the hope that the students will further internalize and model these principles.

USING DRUMS IN THE CLASSROOM

A special group does not have to be formed to realize the benefits of drums in school. General music class percussion ensembles require the same discipline and teamwork to achieve success. If a part is being played in a sloppy manner, we stop playing and clean it up. "Focus" is a key word in prompting the students. The payoff is huge. When a class hits a groove, you can feel the unity, the concentration, the excitement, and the momentum in the room.

Most of the ensembles in this book are aimed at general music classes.

FOSTERING THE CREATIVE

Improvisation, a creative endeavor, is a key element in music education. Drum ensemble provides a golden opportunity to promote improvisational skills. Having students develop their own rhythms to use as the basis for ensemble is another way to foster their creative abilities.

See the Appendix for information on setting up improvisation and building ensembles with student-created rhythms.

THE POWER OF A STRONG MUSIC PROGRAM

A well-balanced general music program can have a powerful growth impact on students. Students will be educated at a profound level by using a varied approach.

SING
SAY (use speech activities for rhythmic training and expressiveness)
DANCE
PLAY (non-pitched percussion, Orff instruments, recorders, etc.)
CREATE

Blend together the development of conceptual understanding and the ability to read notation appropriate for each grade level. Activate the students with music-making! Involve auditory, visual, tactile, and kinesthetic senses, and students will blossom.

Drum ensembles can play a critical role in this varied approach to music education, as well as promote Discipline, Respect, and Unity through Music.

JAM RHYTHMS

- Jam rhythms are rhythms that feel good to play for an extended period of time.

- There is an ensemble for each jam rhythm in the Jam Rhythm Ensembles section of this publication.

- In general, the jam rhythms in this collection progress from simple to complex; however, the order is not exact. Any particular jam rhythm or jam rhythm ensemble may be easy for one group and difficult for another.

- The feeling and difficulty level of a rhythm can be changed dramatically by changing the location of the accents.

- These rhythms can be grouped together in different combinations to form new jam rhythms.

- These rhythms can be used as accompaniments for each other.

- Many of these rhythms have been collected through the years from watching students create their own patterns.

- Have your students create their own jam rhythms. When students add their own ideas, they feel a sense of ownership. This contribution develops their musicianship and heightens their interest and involvement.

- The rhythms of life are infinite. There are many other jam rhythms.

JAM RHYTHM ENSEMBLES

OVERVIEW

- The aim of the jam rhythm ensembles is to provide a collection of materials that elementary and middle school students will perform with intensity and success.

- Many of the ensembles in this collection are intended to be quick studies for the students to succeed in putting the parts together and to enjoy the feeling of the drumming experience. There are also some challenging ensembles that will require extended practice.

THE GROOVE

The most important factor that determines the players' success in an ensemble is whether or not they achieve a groove. The groove brings unity, concentration, and a sense of well-being. The difficulty of the parts is secondary. Focus on the groove.

- The object of performing these ensembles is to "get into a groove." When all parts click and they sink into a tight fit and the ensemble gains a momentum of its own, you are in the groove. The groove gives the players a sense of being part of something much bigger than themselves.

- What to do once the groove is established:

  a) Enjoy it! Let it play for a while without making any changes or additions.
  b) Invite volunteers to improvise. This individual improvisation can be preceded by a group practice in which the teacher plays the main rhythm and students improvise as a group to develop some ideas of what they want to play when it is their turn to improvise.
  c) Have students create a new part or parts to add to the ensemble.

CUSTOMIZING THE ENSEMBLE FOR YOUR PLAYERS

- If a part is too difficult for the whole group to learn, pick an individual who can play it. If that doesn't work, simplify or delete the part. If there are too many parts for the group...delete!

- Instrumentation in the ensemble arrangements is limited to Lead Drum, Bass Drum, Drum #2, Shaker, Cowbell, Claves, Agogo Bell, and/or Guiro. Adapt the instrumentation according to what you have available. Possible instrument substitutions include the following:

    Shakers: maracas, cabasa, shekere, chocallo, multi-guiro

    Cowbell: gankogui, agogo bell, claves, sticks

    Lead Drum: conga drum, tubano, djembé, ashiko, bongos, snare, tom-toms from drum set, five-gallon water jugs turned upside down, hand drum (frame drum)

    Bass Drum: djun djun, surdo, floor tom, bass drum from drum set, tumba (low conga) with mallet, low hand drum (frame drum) with mallet

- If a Drum #2 is placed above the Lead Drum on a score, it should be higher pitched than the Lead Drum. If it is placed below the Lead Drum, it should be lower pitched.

- These ensembles can be played by as few as two or three drums, or by as many as you can get. (I originally started with four drums and slowly accumulated more. We now have 16 plus a contra surdo which we use as our bass.) The more drums you have, the bigger your sound, and the more students you can get involved.

- The teacher should play the Cowbell or Bass Drum parts when necessary to keep the ensemble together.

- Keep in mind that when drums played by hand are mixed with drums played with sticks, the sticks can overpower the hands. Make sure that all parts can be heard.

NOTATION/ROTE

- Elementary and middle school children can play by ear and by rote rhythms that are far more difficult than they can read—and they should have the opportunity to do so. Use speech (words, phrases, or rhythm syllables) and charts with the words to aide this process. See Teaching Suggestions in the Appendix for more information on the teaching process of "speech to body percussion to instruments."

- If you are teaching a jam rhythm ensemble from notation, be sure that it is within the students' rhythm reading arsenal. It is possible to introduce one new element of notation if they are ready for it. Use rhythm syllables when doing this. Introduce it with a drum first to get the rhythm into their ears, then have them echo you with the syllables for the notation.

DIFFICULTY RATINGS

- These ensembles are listed according to <u>approximate</u> difficulty ratings. Use these ratings as a starting point for deciding whom an ensemble is appropriate for, then adjust when necessary. (One year I had a fourth grade class that succeeded only on the second or third grade level material, and another fourth grade class that was ready for special group material.)

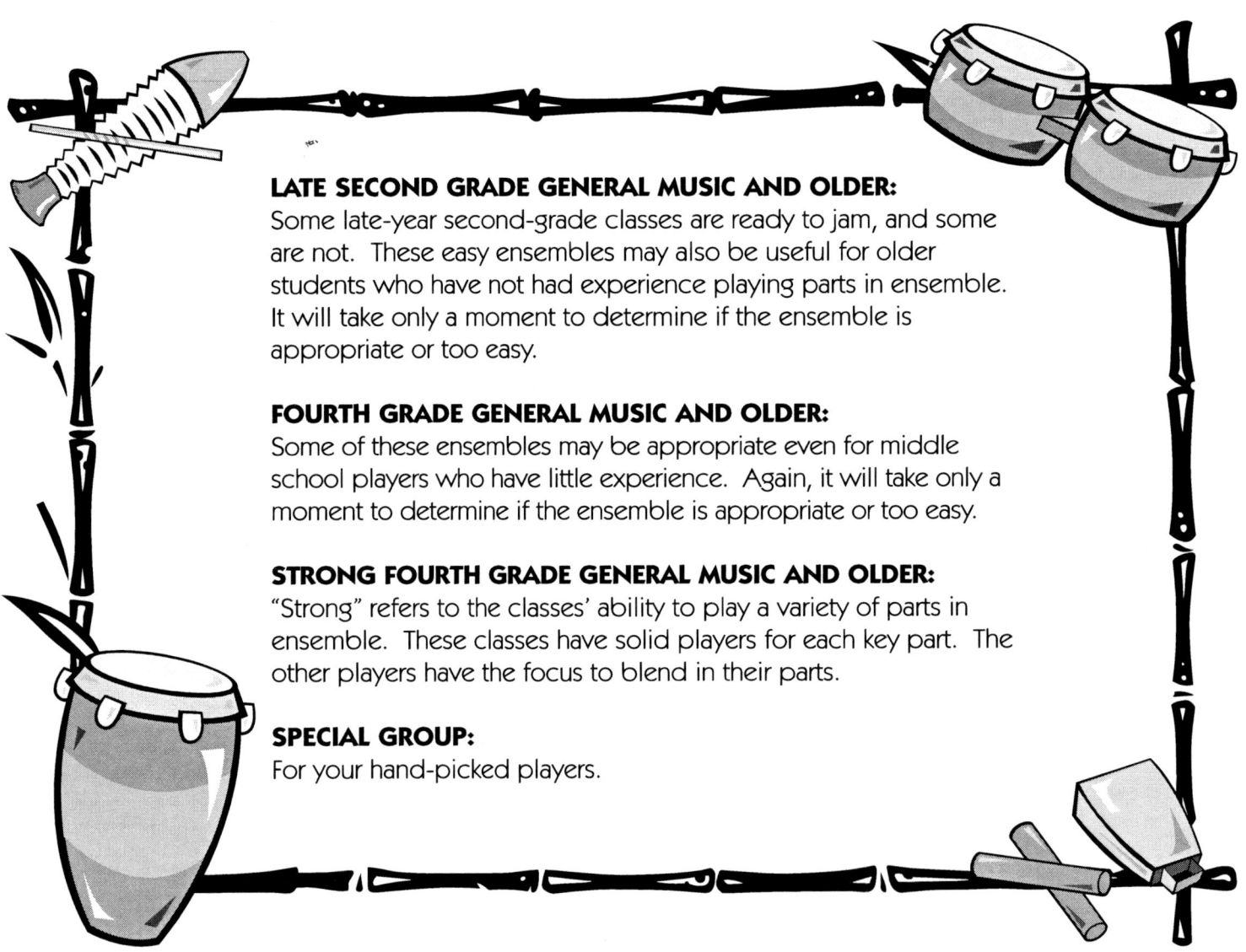

LATE SECOND GRADE GENERAL MUSIC AND OLDER:
Some late-year second-grade classes are ready to jam, and some are not. These easy ensembles may also be useful for older students who have not had experience playing parts in ensemble. It will take only a moment to determine if the ensemble is appropriate or too easy.

FOURTH GRADE GENERAL MUSIC AND OLDER:
Some of these ensembles may be appropriate even for middle school players who have little experience. Again, it will take only a moment to determine if the ensemble is appropriate or too easy.

STRONG FOURTH GRADE GENERAL MUSIC AND OLDER:
"Strong" refers to the classes' ability to play a variety of parts in ensemble. These classes have solid players for each key part. The other players have the focus to blend in their parts.

SPECIAL GROUP:
For your hand-picked players.

JAM RHYTHMS IN 4/4

THESE RHYTHMS APPEAR IN THIS COLLECTION IN ENSEMBLES APPROPRIATE FOR LATE SECOND GRADE AND OLDER

THESE RHYTHMS APPEAR IN THIS COLLECTION IN ENSEMBLES APPROPRIATE FOR FOURTH GRADE AND OLDER

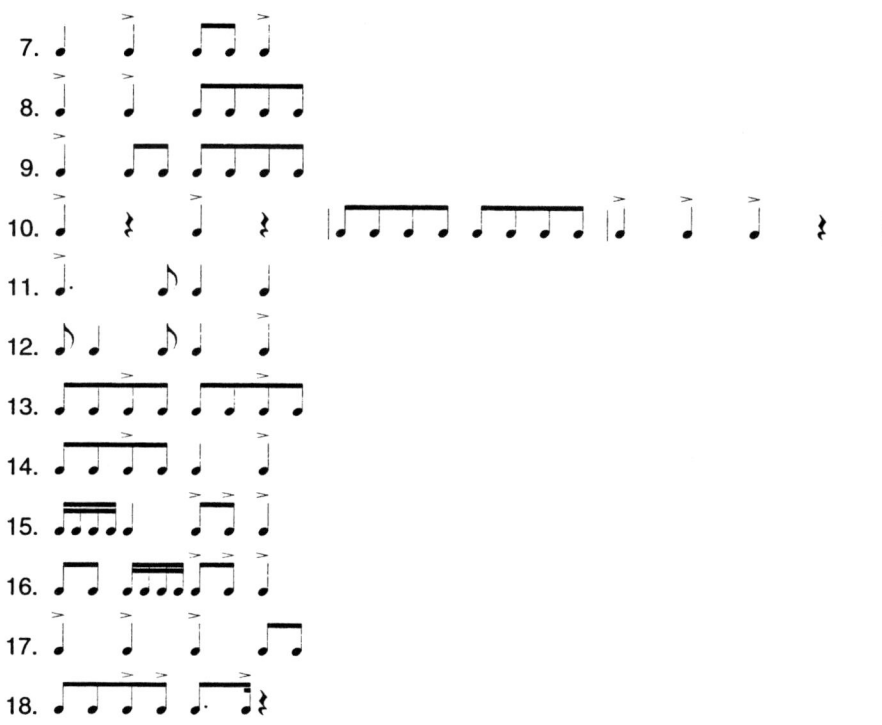

JAM RHYTHMS IN 4/4

> **THESE RHYTHMS APPEAR IN THIS COLLECTION IN ENSEMBLES APPROPRIATE FOR STRONG FOURTH GRADE AND OLDER**

19. – 32. (rhythmic notation)

> **THESE RHYTHMS APPEAR IN THIS COLLECTION IN ENSEMBLES APPROPRIATE FOR SPECIAL GROUPS**

33. – 42. (rhythmic notation)

JAM RHYTHMS IN 4/4

SOME BASIC 4/4 ACCOMPANIMENT PARTS

1. ♩ ♩ ♩ ♩
2. ♩ 𝄽 ♩ 𝄽
3. ♩ 𝄽 —
4. ♩ ♩ ♩ 𝄽
5. ♫♫ ♫♫ ♫♫ ♫♫
6. 𝄽 ♩ 𝄽 ♩
7. 𝄽 ♩ 𝄽 ♫
8. ♬♬ ♬♬ ♬♬ ♬♬
9. ♫ 𝄽 ♫ 𝄽   (difficult, but very exciting)
10. 𝄽 ♫ 𝄽 ♫   (difficult, but very exciting)

JAM RHYTHM ENSEMBLES IN 4/4

LATE SECOND GRADE AND OLDER

1. Shaker
   Lead Drum
   Bass Drum

2. Cowbell
   Lead Drum
   Bass Drum

3. Cowbell
   Lead Drum
   Bass Drum

4. Shaker
   Cowbell
   Lead Drum
   Bass Drum

5. Cowbell
   Lead Drum
   Bass Drum

6. Cowbell
   Lead Drum
   Bass Drum

JAM RHYTHM ENSEMBLES IN 4/4

FOURTH GRADE AND OLDER

7. Shaker / Cowbell / Lead Drum / Bass Drum

8. Cowbell / Guiro / Lead Drum / Bass Drum

9. Shaker / Cowbell / Lead Drum / Bass Drum

a three meas. example

10. Shaker / Cowbell / Lead Drum / Bass Drum

Example 11 is the same figure as Example 1 with accents on 2, 4.

11. Shaker / Guiro / Lead Drum / Bass Drum

12. Shaker / Cowbell / Lead Drum / Bass Drum

JAM RHYTHM ENSEMBLES IN 4/4

13. Shaker
    Cowbell
    Lead Drum
    Bass Drum

14. Cowbell
    Lead Drum
    Drum #2
    Bass Drum

15. Shaker
    Cowbell
    Lead Drum
    Bass Drum

16. Shaker
    Cowbell
    Lead Drum
    Bass Drum

17. Cowbell
    Drum #2
    Lead Drum
    Bass Drum

18. Claves
    Shaker
    Lead Drum
    Bass Drum

    The Conga; lead drum variation:

JAM RHYTHM ENSEMBLES IN 4/4

STRONG FOURTH GRADE AND OLDER

19. Cowbell / Guiro / Lead Drum / Bass Drum

20. Shaker / Cowbell / Lead Drum / Bass Drum

21. Shaker / Cowbell / Lead Drum / Bass Drum

22. Shaker / Cowbell / Lead Drum / Bass Drum

23. Shaker / Cowbell / Lead Drum / Drum #2 / Bass Drum

JAM RHYTHM ENSEMBLES IN 4/4

JAM RHYTHM ENSEMBLES IN 4/4

29. Shaker
    Claves
    Lead Drum
    Bass Drum

30. Shaker
    Cowbell
    Lead Drum
    Bass Drum

31. Shaker
    Cowbell
    Lead Drum
    Bass Drum

32. Shaker
    Agogo Bell
    Lead Drum
    Drum #2
    Bass Drum

    (A Samba—add Drum #2 last)

JAM RHYTHM ENSEMBLES IN 4/4

SPECIAL GROUPS

33. Shaker / Cowbell / Lead Drum / Bass Drum

Example 34 is the same figure as Example 10 with accents on 1, 3.

34.

35.

36.

37.

JAM RHYTHM ENSEMBLES IN 4/4

38. Shaker / Cowbell / Lead Drum / Bass Drum

39. Shaker / Cowbell / Lead Drum / Bass Drum

Example 40 is the same figure as Examples 10 and 34 with accents on 1 + 3.

40. Claves / Shaker / Drum #2 / Lead Drum / Bass Drum

41. Shaker / Cowbell / Lead Drum / Bass Drum

(lead drum variation:)

42. Cowbell / Drum #2 / Lead Drum / Bass Drum

JAM RHYTHMS IN 6/8

6/8 is a wonderful meter throughout the elementary school years for developing a strong sense of the "heartbeat" (steady beat), duple meter, movement, vocal expression with rhymes, and so on. It is a more difficult meter for young players to play on drums because the accents shift back and forth when playing continual eighth notes. With practice, your capable fourth graders and beyond can develop the ability.

The pattern shown above is an African "Mother Rhythm." It is possibly the most significant 6/8 pattern listed. Practicing this rhythm will accelerate your drummers' development. It can be used as an accompaniment with any of the other rhythms listed. Its momentum is unrelenting.

THESE RHYTHMS APPEAR IN THIS COLLECTION IN ENSEMBLES APPROPRIATE FOR FOURTH GRADE AND OLDER

1.
2.
3.

THESE RHYTHMS APPEAR IN THIS COLLECTION IN ENSEMBLES APPROPRIATE FOR STRONG FOURTH GRADE AND OLDER

4.
5.
6.
7.

JAM RHYTHMS IN 6/8

THESE RHYTHMS APPEAR IN THIS COLLECTION IN ENSEMBLES APPROPRIATE FOR SPECIAL GROUPS

8. ♩ ♪ ♩ ♪
9. ♩ ♪ ♩ ♪
10. ♩. ♩. | ♩. ♫ |
11. ♩ ♪ ♫
   R R L R L

SOME BASIC 6/8 ACCOMPANIMENT PARTS

1. ♩. 𝄽.
2. ♩. ♩.
3. ♩. ♩. | ♩. ♩. |
4. ♩. ♩. | ♩. 𝄽. |
5. ♫ ♩.
6. ♩. ♫
7. ♫ ♫

JAM RHYTHM ENSEMBLES IN 6/8

FOURTH GRADE AND OLDER

1. Shaker
   Cowbell
   Lead Drum
   Bass Drum

2. Shaker
   Cowbell
   Lead Drum
   Bass Drum

3. Cowbell
   Lead Drum
   Bass Drum

   (Lead Drum requires alternation of hands)

JAM RHYTHM ENSEMBLES IN 6/8

STRONG FOURTH GRADE AND OLDER

4.
Shaker	♩. ♩.	♩. ♩.
Cowbell	♩ ♪ ♩.	♩. ♩.
Lead Drum	♫♪ ♩ ♪	♩ ♪ ♩ ♪
Bass Drum	♩. ♩.	♩. 𝄽.

5.
Shaker	♩. ♩.	♩. ♩.
Drum #2	>♩ ♪ ♩.	—
Lead Drum	♩ ♪ ♩ ♪	♫♪ ♩ ♪
Bass Drum	♩. 𝄽.	♩. 𝄽.

6.
Shaker	♩. ♩.	♩. 𝄽.
Cowbell	♩ ♪ ♩.	♩ ♪ ♩.
Lead Drum	♩ ♪ ♩ ♪	♩ ♪ ♫♪
Bass Drum	>♩. ♩.	♩. ♩.

7.
Shaker	♩. 𝄽.	♩. 𝄽.
Cowbell	♩ ♪ ♩.	♩ ♪ ♩.
Lead Drum	>♩. ♩.	>♫♪ ♩.
Bass Drum	♩. ♩.	♩. 𝄽.

JAM RHYTHM ENSEMBLES IN 6/8

SPECIAL GROUPS

Example 8 is the same figure as Examples 3 and 9, but with accents on 1, 6.

8. Shaker
   Drum #2
   Lead Drum
   Bass Drum

Example 9 is the same figure as Examples 3 and 8, but with accents on 1, 3.

9. Cowbell
   Drum #2
   Lead Drum
   Bass Drum
   (simplified Cowbell:)

10. Cowbell
    Drum #2
    Lead Drum
    Bass Drum
    (simplified Cowbell:)

11. Cowbell
    Drum #2
    Lead Drum
    Bass Drum
    (simplified Cowbell:)

    (Lead Drum hand alternation RRLRL)

JAM RHYTHMS IN 3/4

THIS RHYTHM APPEARS IN THIS COLLECTION IN AN ENSEMBLE APPROPRIATE FOR LATE SECOND GRADE AND OLDER

1. [notation]

THESE RHYTHMS APPEAR IN THIS COLLECTION IN ENSEMBLES APPROPRIATE FOR FOURTH GRADE AND OLDER

2. [notation]
3. [notation]

THESE RHYTHMS APPEAR IN THIS COLLECTION IN ENSEMBLES APPROPRIATE FOR STRONG FOURTH GRADE AND OLDER

4. [notation]
5. [notation]
6. [notation]

THIS RHYTHM APPEARS IN THIS COLLECTION IN AN ENSEMBLE APPROPRIATE FOR SPECIAL GROUPS

7. [notation]

JAM RHYTHMS IN 3/4

SOME BASIC 3/4 ACCOMPANIMENT PARTS

1. ♩ 𝄽 𝄽
2. ♩ ♩ ♩
3. ♩ 𝄽 ♩
4. ♫ ♫ ♫
5. ♬♬ ♬♬ ♬♬

JAM RHYTHM ENSEMBLES IN 3/4

LATE SECOND GRADE AND OLDER

1. Shaker
   Lead Drum
   Bass Drum

   (simplify Bass Drum to continual ♩ 𝄽 𝄽 for 2nd)

FOURTH GRADE AND OLDER

2. Shaker
   Lead Drum
   Bass Drum

3. Shaker
   Cowbell
   Lead Drum
   Bass Drum

JAM RHYTHM ENSEMBLES IN 3/4

STRONG FOURTH GRADE AND OLDER

4. Cowbell
   Lead Drum
   Bass Drum

5. Shaker
   Cowbell
   Lead Drum
   Bass Drum

6. Shaker
   Cowbell
   Lead Drum
   Bass Drum

SPECIAL GROUPS

7. Shaker
   Cowbell
   Lead Drum
   Bass Drum

ENSEMBLES BASED ON SPEECH

MONKEY MONKEY MOO

Traditional
Arranged by Jim Solomon

Recommended grade level: 2nd, 3rd

♩ = 92 ~ 108

T = Tone (Open tone) B = Bass

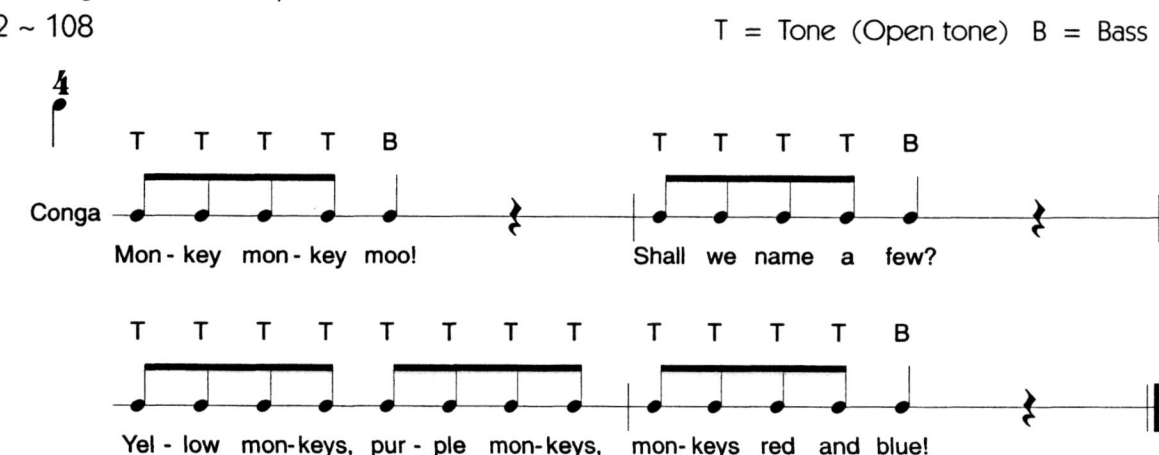

FORM:

A Section - Play all parts 1x
B Section - Only accompanying parts play
  (use "inner hearing" to know when Ratchet, Vibraslap, and Cymbal play)
A Section - Play all parts 1x

Another option for the form is to have all parts played 2x or 4x, then use accompanying parts 1x as an interlude before repeating all parts again.

ACCOMPANYING PARTS:

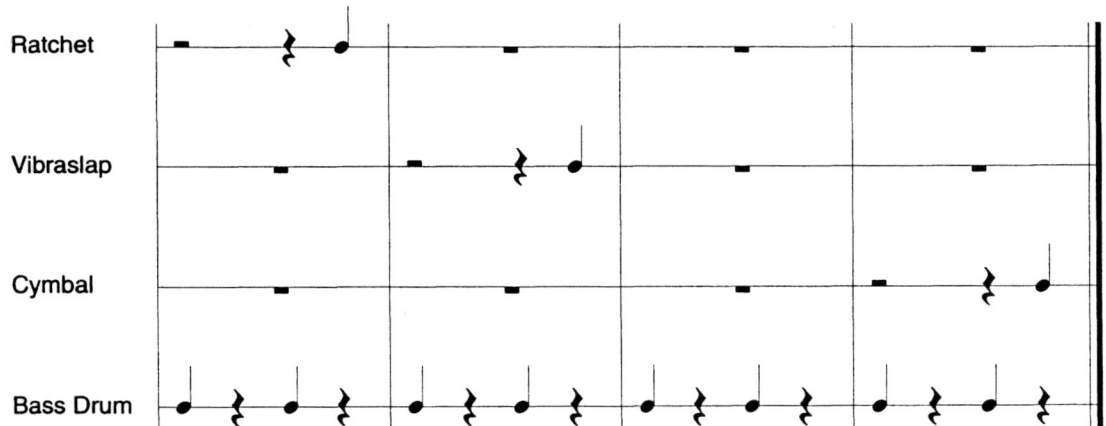

TEACHING SUGGESTIONS:

Rhythm of Rhyme: 1) Ask students what colors they hear, then speak the rhyme. 2) Show a chart. Mark words where bass is played with a "B." Speak rhyme again and clap on basses. 3) Students speak rhyme and clap on basses. 4) Patsch rhythm of entire rhyme. 5) Play on drums.

Play Ratchet on first rest in the rhyme, Vibraslap on the second rest, and Cymbal on the last rest.

When students are secure with the rhythm, teacher can add Cowbell: ♩ ♫ ♩ ♫

ENSEMBLES BASED ON SPEECH

PIGS LIKE MUD

Traditional
Arranged by Jim Solomon

Recommended grade level: 2nd, 3rd

♩ = 120 ~ 144

T = Tone (Open tone) B = Bass

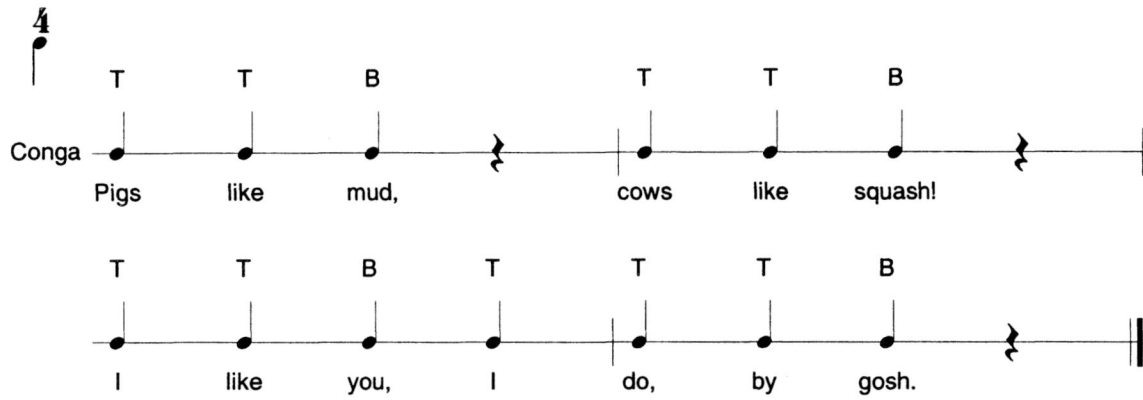

FORM:

A Section - Play 4x
B Section - Soloists play (improvise or play the basic rhythm of the words, whichever the group is ready for)
A Section - Play 4x

ACCOMPANYING PARTS:

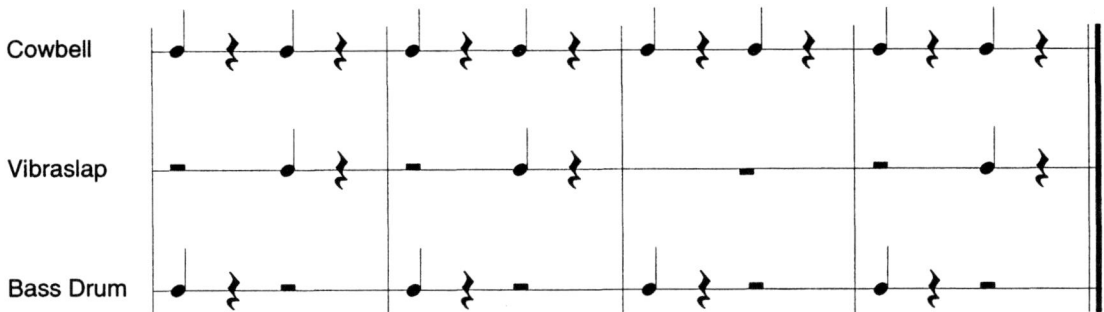

TEACHING SUGGESTIONS:

1) Use a chart. Mark words where bass is played with a "B." Teach location of basses first by speaking rhyme and clapping on basses. 2) Play rhythm of entire rhyme.

Play Vibraslap only on special words "mud," "squash," and "gosh."

| ENSEMBLES BASED ON SPEECH |

TINY SURFER

Traditional
Arranged by Jim Solomon

Recommended grade level: 2nd, 3rd, and 4th

♩ = 100 ~ 112

T = Tone (Open tone)   B = Bass

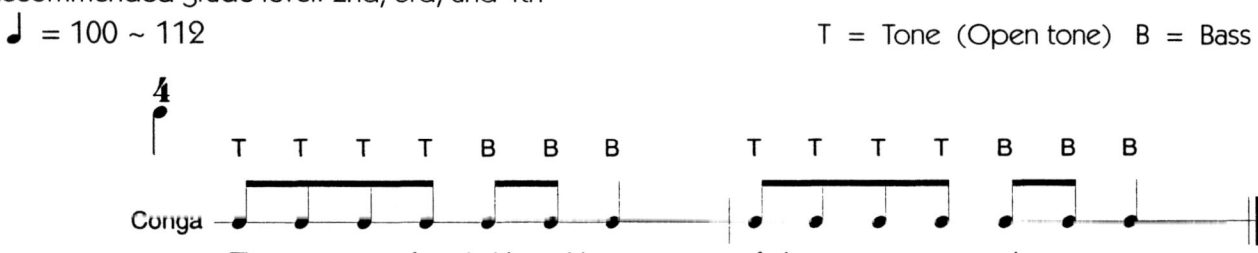

FORM:

A Section - Play 2x
B Section - Accompanying parts 2x
A Section - Repeat

Have students suggest their own form.

ACCOMPANYING PARTS:

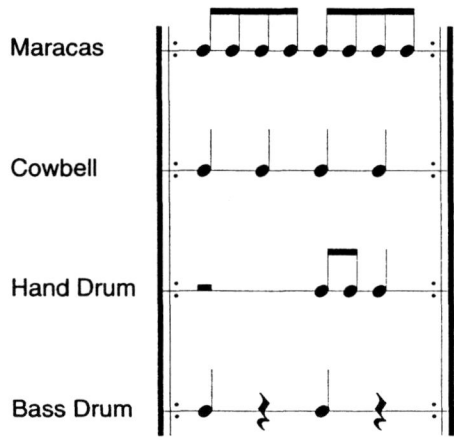

ENSEMBLES BASED ON SPEECH

ORDER IN THE GALLERY!

Traditional
Arranged by Jim Solomon

Recommended grade level: 4th and older

♩ = 116 ~ 132   T = Tone (Open tone)   B = Bass

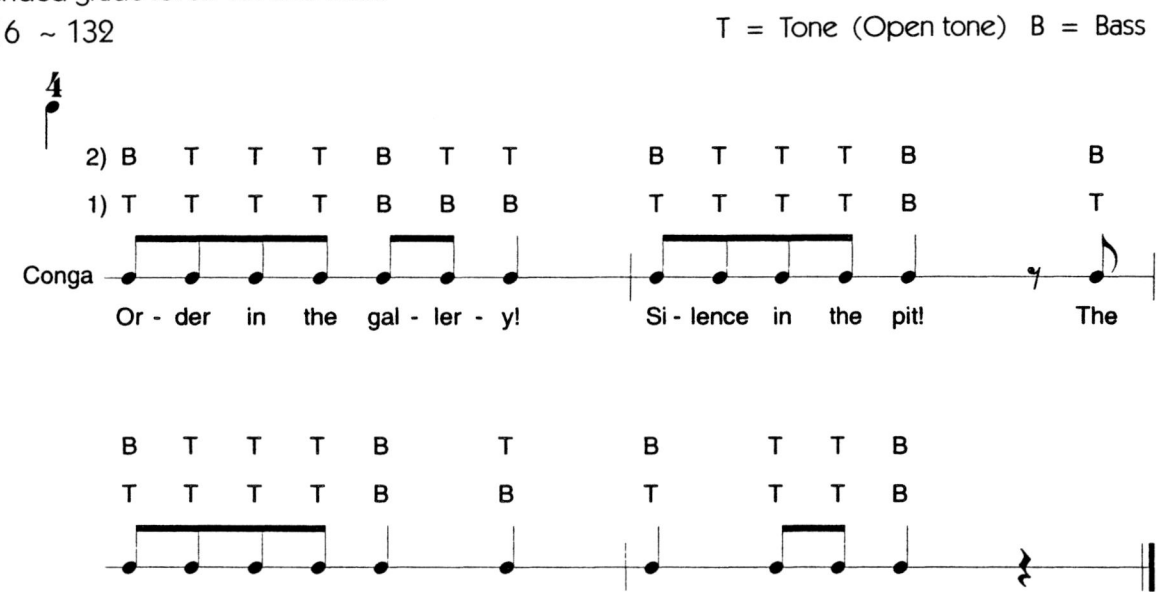

Two options are given above for alternation of Tone and Bass on Conga Drum (or for the alternation of the accents on another drum). Number two is more challenging and more "hip."

FORM:

- A Section - Play 2x with all parts
- B Section - Bongos improvise 2x through with accompanying parts
- A Section - Repeat
- B Section - Repeat
- A Section - Repeat

ACCOMPANYING PARTS:

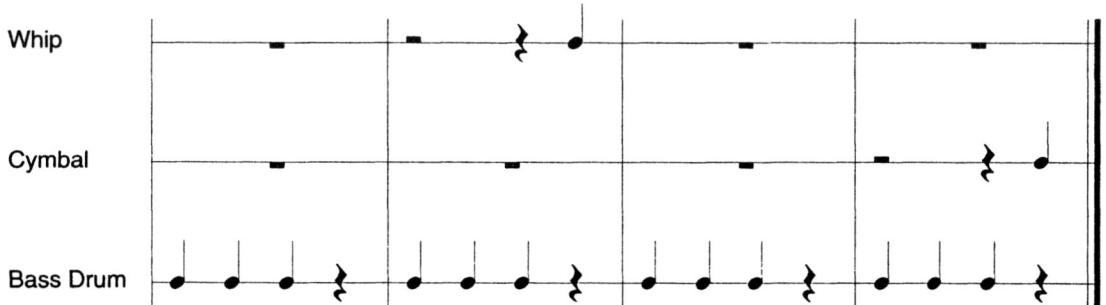

TEACHING SUGGESTIONS:

Rhythm of Rhyme: 1) Prep the anacrusis: count 4s, clap on "1." 2) Tell students to find the word at the beginning of one of the sentences that starts before beat "1." 3) Teacher speaks rhyme, students identify "The." 4) Practice "The people in the boxes" with patschen. 5) Speak and patsch whole rhyme. 6) Tap floor on "Basses." 7) Patsch the "Tones" and tap knee on "Basses."

The Whip plays on the first rest in the rhyme, the Cymbal plays on the second.

ENSEMBLES BASED ON SPEECH

PETER, PETER IF YOU'RE ABLE

Traditional
Arranged by Jim Solomon

Recommended grade level: 4th and older

♩ = 104 ~ 116

T = Tone (Open tone)   B = Bass

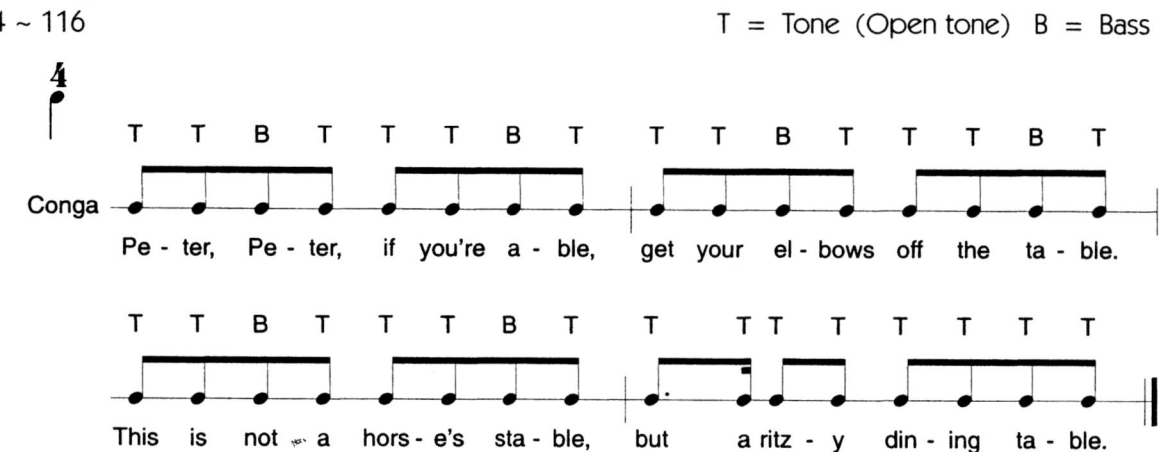

FORM:

Introduction - Layer instruments in 2-measure intervals: 1) Guiro 2) Cowbell 3) Maracas 4) Bass Drum
A Section -   Play 4x
B Section -   Improvise with accompanying parts
A Section -   Repeat
B Section -   Repeat
A Section -   Repeat with Cowbell pattern #2

ACCOMPANYING PARTS:

TEACHING SUGGESTIONS:

Rhythm of Rhyme: 1) Teach rhythm of 4th measure first. All instruments will play in unison on 4th measure.

ENSEMBLES BASED ON SPEECH

IF YOU SEE A MONKEY

Traditional
Arranged by Jim Solomon

Recommended grade level: 4th and older.
♩ = 88 ~ 108

T = Tone (Open tone)   B = Bass

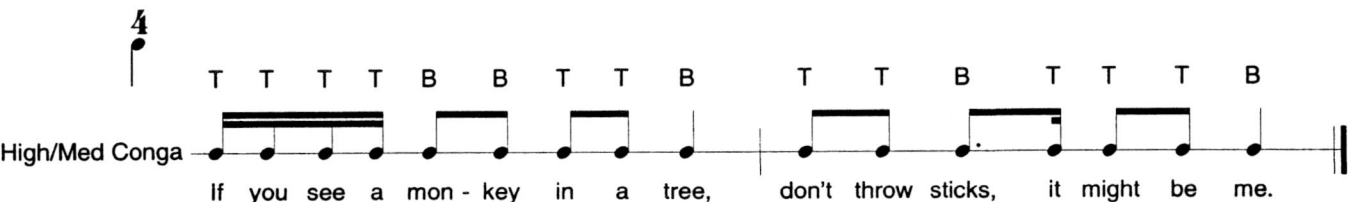

FORM:

A Section -   Play all parts 4x
Interlude -   Accompanying parts play 4 measures
A Section -   Repeat
Interlude -   Repeat
A Section -   Repeat

ACCOMPANYING PARTS:

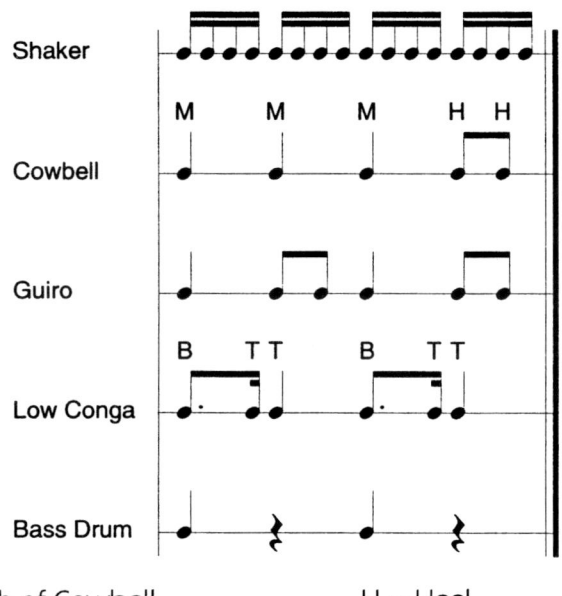

M = Mouth of Cowbell   H = Heel

TEACHING SUGGESTIONS:

Rhythm of Rhyme: 1) Play the rhythm on a drum before telling students the words. 2) Speak rhyme while clapping on the basses. 3) Have students clap basses with you. 4) Echo patsch rhythm of words. 5) Patsch the tones, tap knee on basses. Add Drum #2 after all other parts are done.

ENSEMBLES BASED ON SPEECH

SODA POP

Traditional
Arranged by Jim Solomon

Recommended grade level: 4th and older

♩. = 116 ~ 126

T = Tone (Open tone)   B = Bass

Conga

B T T T | B T T | B T T T | B T T
Pep - si Co - la went to town, Co - ca Co - la shot him down.

B T T T | B T T | B T T T T T | T T. T
Doc - tor Pep - per fixed him up, while drink - ing a bot - tle of Sev - en - Up.

FORM:

Introduction - Bass drum and vibraslap 8 meas.
A Section -   All instruments 2x
Interlude -   Cowbell 8 meas.
A Section -   Repeat

Work with students to add to the form. Include improvisation, other interludes, etc.

ACCOMPANYING PARTS:

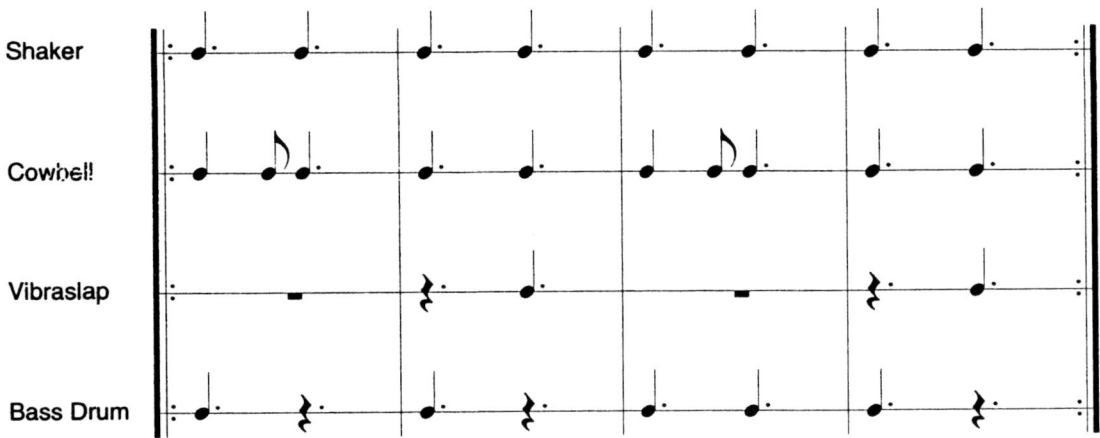

TEACHING SUGGESTIONS:

1) "Listen for the different types of soda pop." Teacher speaks rhyme, students identify. 2) Teacher speaks again and claps on basses. 3) Students speak and clap on basses. 4) Echo patsch rhythm 2 meas. at a time. 5) Patsch rhythm whole rhyme.
6) Patsch rhythm and tap knee on basses. 7) Play on drums.

ENSEMBLES BASED ON SPEECH

OLD JOHN TUCKER

Traditional
Arranged by Jim Solomon

Recommended grade level: 5th and older
♩ = 104 ~ 120   T = Tone (Open tone)   B = Bass

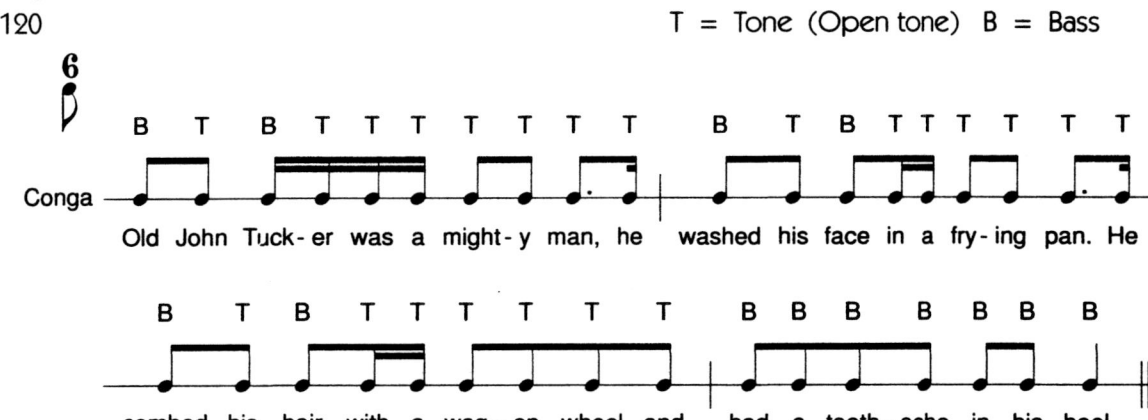

Old John Tuck-er was a might-y man, he washed his face in a fry-ing pan. He combed his hair with a wag-on wheel and had a tooth-ache in his heel.

FORM:

A Section - Congas only, play 1x
Interlude #1 - Cowbell 2 meas.
A¹ -   Congas, Cowbell 1x
Interlude #2 - Maracas 2 meas.
A² -   Congas, Cowbell, Maracas, 1x
Interlude #3 - Drum #2 2 meas.
A³ -   Congas, Cowbell, Maracas, Drum #2 1x
Interlude #4 - Bass Drum 2 meas.
A⁴ -   Congas, Cowbell, Maracas, Drum #2, Bass Drum 1x
A⁴ -   Repeat
A⁴ -   Repeat
A⁴ -   Repeat

ACCOMPANYING PARTS:

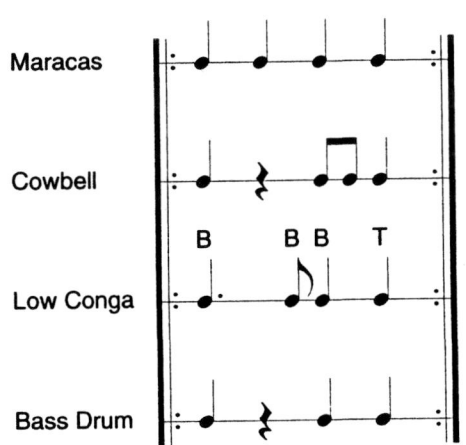

TEACHING SUGGESTIONS:

Rhythm of Rhyme: 1) "I have a tall tale for you. Listen for three unusual things about Old John Tucker." Teacher speaks rhyme, students answer question. 2) Show chart, echo speak one line at a time. Pay close attention to "And" as an eighth note (not 16th note). 3) "Look for where the Basses are." Teacher plays on drum. 4) Teacher plays again, students clap on basses. Play again, students tap knee on Basses. 5) Echo patsch rhythm one phrase at a time. 6) Echo patsch rhythm with Basses included. 7) Patsch rhythm of rhyme. 8) Play on drums.

ENSEMBLES BASED ON SPEECH

DR. FELL

Traditional
Arranged by Jim Solomon

Recommended grade level: 5th or older
♩. = 116 ~ 132

T = Tone (Open tone) B = Bass

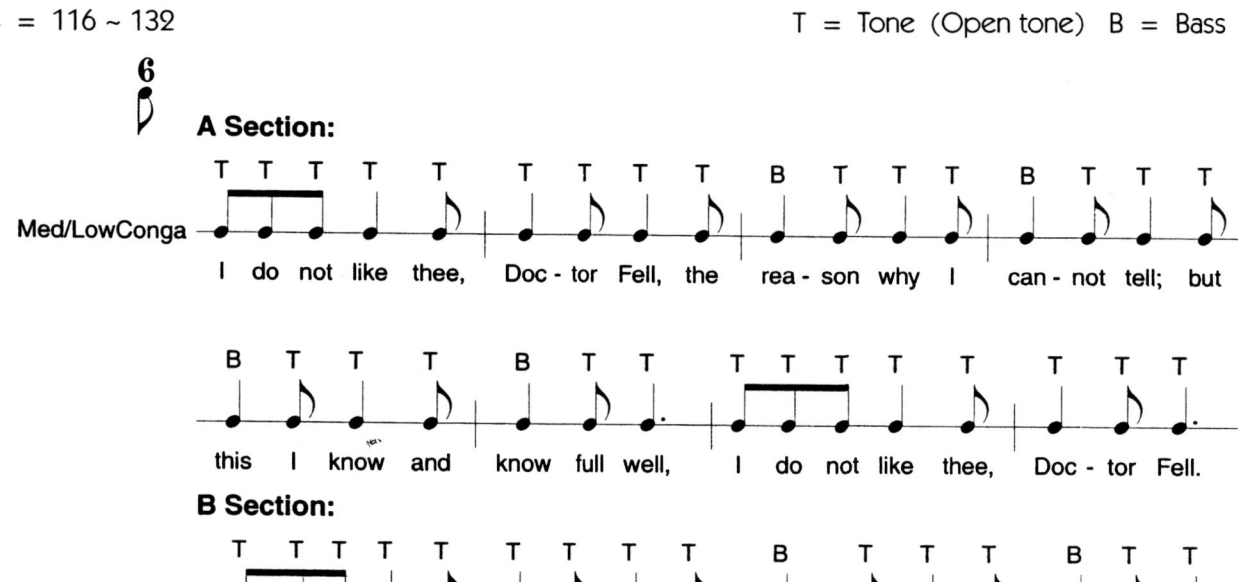

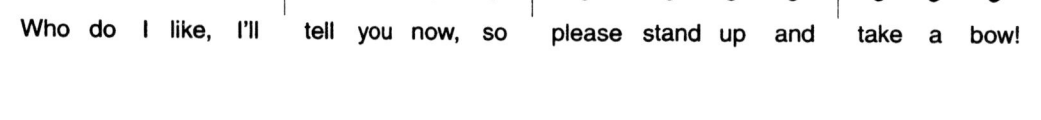

(rhythm of this line to be determined by names of students filled in)

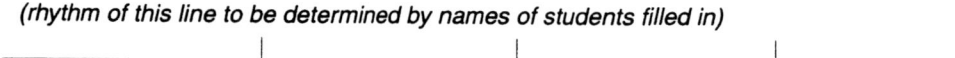

FORM:

A Section - Play 1x, all parts
B Section - Play 1x, all parts, with selected names inserted
Interlude - Cowbell and Drum #2 play 8 meas.
A Section - Repeat
B Section - Repeat

ACCOMPANYING PARTS:

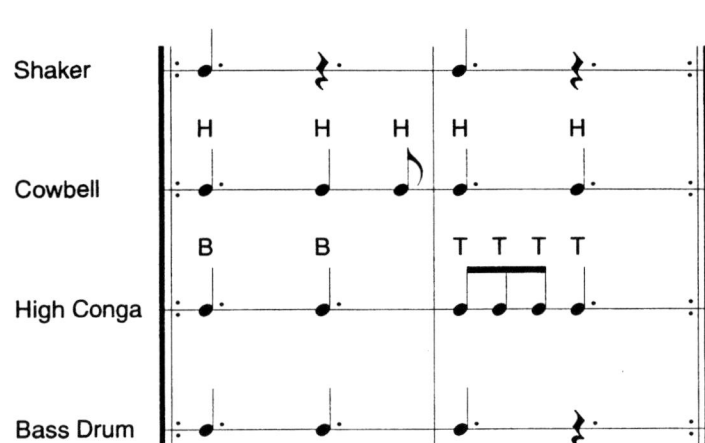

TEACHING SUGGESTIONS:

Use "Dr. Fell" to have students create their own rhythms in 6/8 using their names. They choose students' names in their class to put in the last line, then test the rhythm by speaking the names in order and seeing if it is playable—if it flows. Once the class has arrived at a suitable order of names, have them decide where the basses should be played. Rhythm of Rhyme: 1) Introduce the rhyme by speaking it (with a "firm tone of voice") and inserting the first names of eight students sitting next to each other. Then speak it with eight different names inserted. 2) Echo speak, being sure to make the rhythm of the words, "I do not like thee, Dr. Fell," and "Who do I like, I'll tell you now," very precise.

ENSEMBLES BASED ON SPEECH

RIQUE, RIQUE, RIQUE, RAN

Traditional
Arranged by Jim Solomon

Recommended grade level: 5th or older

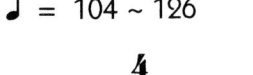   T = Tone (Open tone)   B = Bass

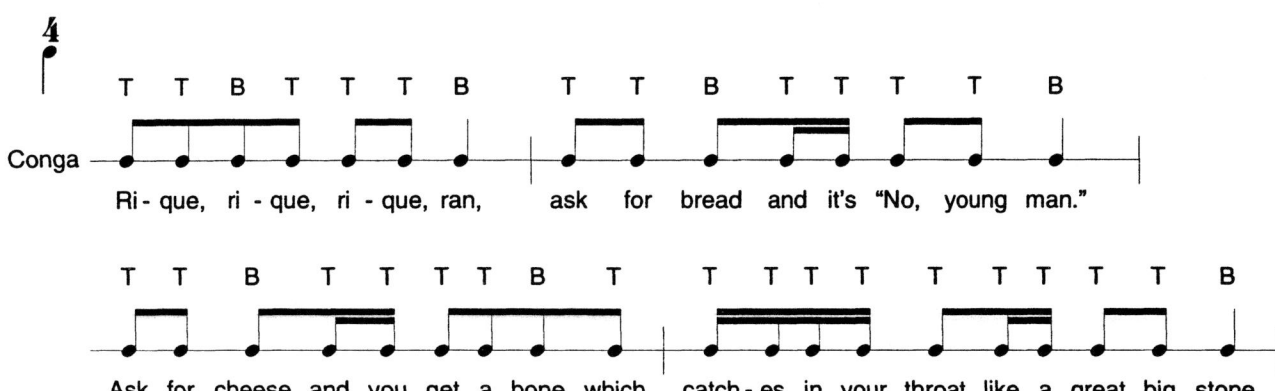

FORM:

A Section - All instruments 2x
B Section - Question/Answer improvisation between conga and bongos
A Section - Repeat
B Section - Repeat
A Section - Repeat

ACCOMPANYING PARTS:

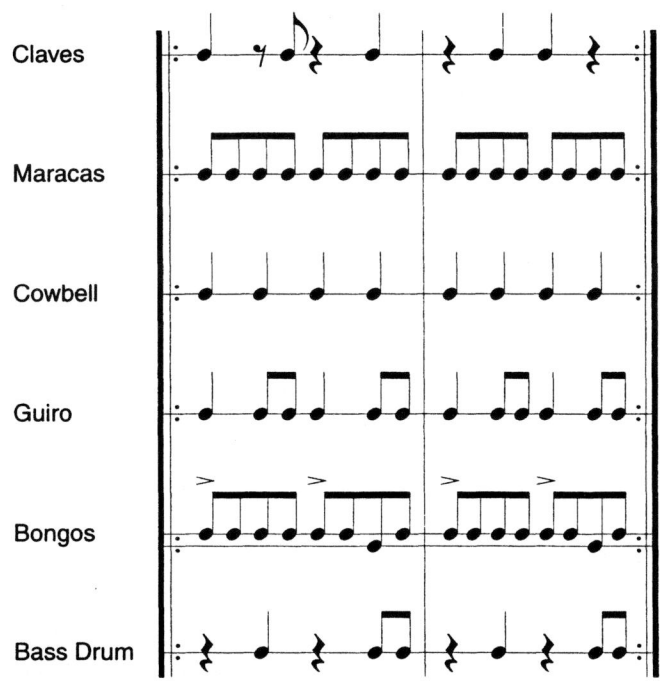

TEACHING SUGGESTIONS:

Rhythm of Rhyme: 1) Speak words, clap on basses. 2) Speak words again, students clap on basses with you. 3) Echo speak words with close attention to pronunciation. 4) Echo patsch rhythm of words. 5) Patsch rhythm of whole rhyme. 6) Patsch tones, tap knee on basses. 7) Play on congas.

ENSEMBLES BASED ON SPEECH

JACK BE NIMBLE
Traditional
Arranged by Jim Solomon

Recommended grade levels: 5th and older (The main rhythm can be played by younger grades, but the accompanying parts and the Form add complexity.)

♩. = 120 ~ 138

T = Tone (Open tone)   B = Bass

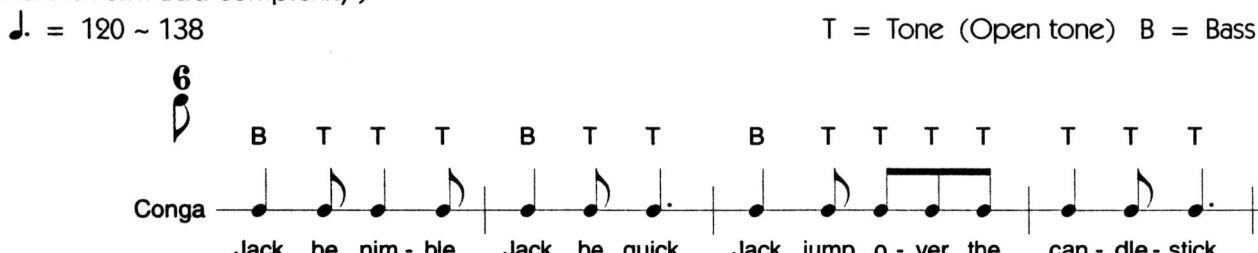

FORM:

Introduction - Layer in: Bongos, 4 meas.
                      add Low Conga, 4 meas.
                      add Bass Drum, 4 meas.
                      add Cowbell, 4 meas.
A Section - Main rhythm with all instruments 8x through
Interlude - Fake ending: all instruments stop 4 meas.
A Section - Repeat (main rhythm stops after 8th time)
Coda - Layer out: stop playing in the reverse order of the entrance, i.e.,
                      Cowbell
                      Bass Drum
                      Low Conga
                      Bongos

ACCOMPANYING PARTS:

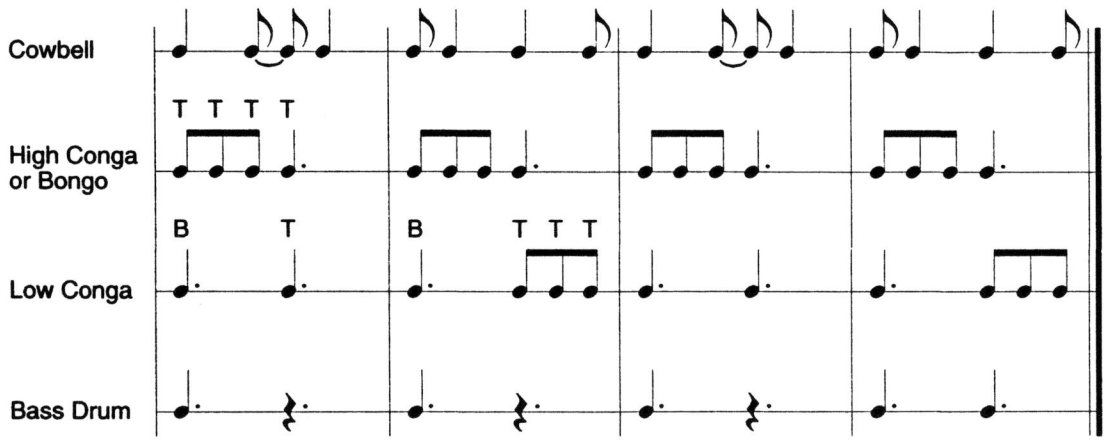

TEACHING SUGGESTIONS:

Rhythm of Rhyme: 1) Before speaking the rhyme, play it on a conga. Then tell the class that the rhythm comes from a rhyme they have all known for years. 2) Clap hands on every "Jack" as teacher speaks rhyme. (These are the Basses.) 3) Patsch rhythm. 4) Patsch rhythm and tap knee on Basses. 5) Play on drums.

ENSEMBLES BASED ON SPEECH

AWAKE, ARISE

Traditional
Arranged by Jim Solomon

Recommended grade level: 5th and older
♩ = 132~152

T = Tone (Open tone) B = Bass

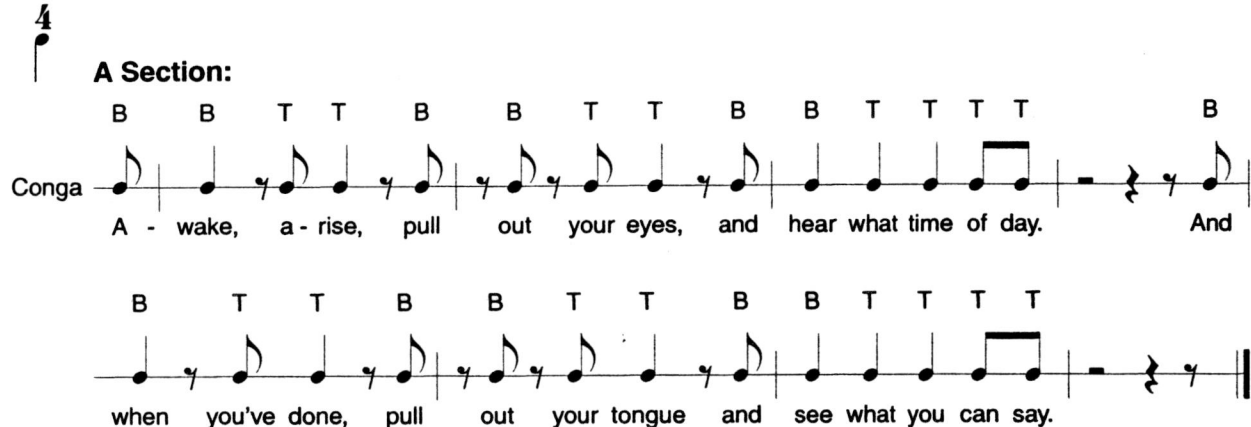

A Section:

Conga: A-wake, a-rise, pull out your eyes, and hear what time of day. And when you've done, pull out your tongue and see what you can say.

B Section:
Individual drummers improvise over this Bass Drum part, maracas continue.

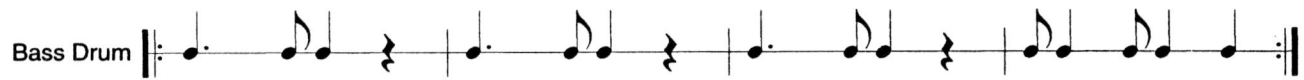

FORM:

Introduction - Bass Drum 4 meas.
A Section - Play 2x, all instruments
B Section - Individual drummers improvise over the new Bass Drum part
A Section - Repeat
B Section - Repeat
A Section - Repeat

ACCOMPANYING PARTS:

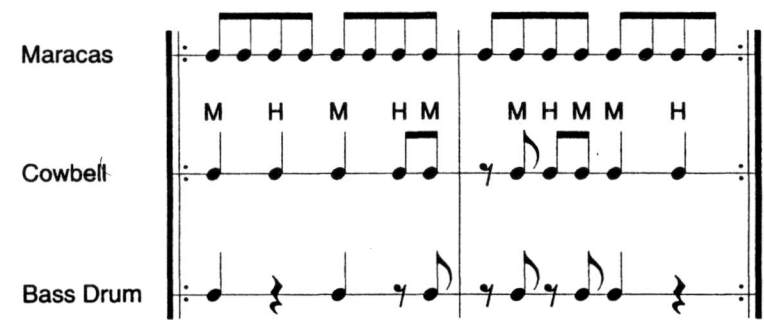

TEACHING SUGGESTIONS:

Rhythm of Rhyme: 1) "I have a strange rhyme for you, but first just listen." Play bass drum part repeatedly so students hear the syncopation and get the feel of it, then speak the words of the rhyme while continuing the bass drum part. 2) Discuss nonsense nature of rhyme. 3) Show chart with words—they read silently while you read aloud (and play the bass drum part). 4) Echo speak phrases while playing the bass drum part. 5) Students read whole rhyme (with bass drum part). 6) Play on drums.

A technique to use with this bass drum pattern is to dampen the head with your free hand on every rest in the pattern. This dampening is very effective in the rhythm if it becomes audible.

APPENDIX

FORM

The form suggestions in these speech pieces are just that. Base your final form on what your students can do. Have your group help develop it. Play with it! Below are some ways in which you can develop the form.

- layer in parts in the introduction
- layer in parts throughout the piece—make the entire arrangement additive
- start together
- insert improvisation sections
- insert solo breaks/group breaks (interludes) in which a specific part is continued or a new part is inserted
- extend the length
- shorten the length
- create unison sections
- jam continuously
- develop a rondo
- repeat one section but not another (A A B A A B)
- insert fake endings (all stop for 8 beats)
- intensify the cowbell part in the final sections(s)
- accelerate to the end in the final section

IMPROVISATION

Improvisation can be set up in many different ways. However, it is helpful to first have the students practice improvising in a group setting. This allows them to develop their ideas and become comfortable without being put on the spot to solo immediately.

HOW LONG SHOULD EACH PLAYER IMPROVISE?

A. Free form with no set phrase length
    Play until appropriate ending is "felt." In the ensembles in this book, this might be appropriate if used as an intro if clear tempo and cues are given for the group to enter. This can also be used as a Coda.

B. Phrase length: "Question and Answer"
    One player asks a question (plays a phrase length rhythm), and a different player gives an answer (responds by playing a phrase-length pattern that relates to the first). This can be continued by two, four, or eight players for the duration of a section.

    Q/A can be structured in different ways:

    - 8-beat question, 7-beat answer

    - 8-beat question, 8-beat answer

    - Question & answer overlap each other's phrases and players can "comment" (fill in) while the other is playing

    - Constant give and take between two players throughout an entire section

    - One player can answer his/her own question (this can eventually lead to an individual improvising throughout an entire section)

C. An entire section, i.e., the B Section, the C Section, etc.

IMPROVISATION REQUIRES PRACTICE!

Set your improvisation sections up to take advantage of the talents and interests of the members of your group.

TEACHING SUGGESTIONS

The use of vocalization to learn rhythm is a worldwide phenomenon. It is said that "If you can say it, you can play it." Basing rhythm ensembles on rhymes and creating words that fit rhythms follow in this tradition. The following formula is extremely successful for teaching many rhythms and accompanying parts:

1) SPEECH   to   **2) BODY PERCUSSION**   to   **3) INSTRUMENTS**

1) Speak words, syllables, or phrases that fit the rhythm.

2) Play the rhythm with body percussion.
   - Some basic types of body percussion are snapping, clapping, patschen (slapping or tapping thighs), and stamping.
   - Echo play: Students echo phrases that the teacher performs using body percussion; listen for accuracy.
   - Mimic the motion of the instrument that will be used.

3) Play the rhythm on instruments.

This formula progresses in levels of difficulty. Speech is the easiest. Body percussion requires physical coordination. Instruments require physical coordination and manipulation of physical objects. You will not know for sure if a student can play a part on an instrument until you actually see him/her playing the instrument.

If a piece is learned from notation rather than a rhyme, first read with rhythm syllables, then use body percussion to practice the parts. If the rhythms are too difficult for the students to read with rhythm syllables, echo play the rhythms with body percussion first. Words that fit the rhythms can be created (by teacher and students) for any parts that the students are having difficulty grasping.

Visualization (use of charts, other visuals, written notation) can expedite the learning process and memorization of parts. It is strongly recommended to use charts of the rhymes for teaching the Ensembles Based on Speech.

TEACHING SUGGESTIONS CONTINUED

TOTALITY FIRST

It is important that students hear the main rhythm or rhyme of a piece before learning individual parts. Then start working on the most difficult parts first, allowing the players more time to practice those parts. It is also important to allow practice time for the easier parts with which all students will experience success.

TRYOUTS

Have practice times (which are actually unannounced "tryouts") where you watch groups of students take turns practicing particular parts on the instruments. Observe them as they play and make notes as to which students can perform each part. After completing the tryouts (particularly for the most difficult parts), you can select players and balance the ensemble with strong players at the critical positions along with other students who will be able to play their parts if they have a strong player beside them. (Author's note: I usually select students for specific parts after the students leave class. In the next class period, I quietly assign students to the most critical instrument parts. This is a kinder approach than watching students practice a part and then immediately announcing who got the part.)

Some teachers have remarked that their students do not like nursery rhymes. If you feel your students won't react positively to an ensemble based on a rhyme, introduce the rhyme in a different way; play the rhythm on a drum. After they have heard the rhythm from a drum, echo play the phrases and remark, "Did you know that this rhythm comes from a simple rhyme? When you know the rhyme, it is easier to play the piece. People all over the world learn rhythms this way."

BUILDING AN ENSEMBLE WITH STUDENT-CREATED RHYTHMS

Teachers can provide opportunities for students to develop their own percussion ensembles. Below are some easy steps to help students develop these arrangements.

1) Start with a Jam Rhythm or a rhythm given by a student.

2) Class practices main rhythm with body percussion and/or instruments.

3) Teacher challenges the class to play something different from the main rhythm. It sometimes helps to clarify this further by asking for something that will fit or something that will help the feeling of the rhythm. Students make up accompanying parts using body percussion or instruments. NOTE: This will sound chaotic because everyone is playing something different. That's okay! The creative process is rarely neat and tidy. (If students randomly play ideas that do not relate to the main rhythm, it is helpful for the teacher to demonstrate a variety of ideas that both fit and do not fit and to ask the students to evaluate.)

5) Observe the students closely to see who is playing an appropriate pattern they can repeat.

6) Have some students play their parts, ask who wants to join them, and decide on instruments to assign to the new parts.

7) Add new parts one at a time to the main rhythm, and let each stabilize before adding more parts.

APPENDIX

INSTRUMENT TECHNIQUE

The goal of this book regarding technique is to describe how upper-elementary and middle school students can successfully use the instruments as they would be used in these ensembles. There are many other possibilities regarding technique for the instruments discussed.

When working with elementary and middle school students, the dominant hand can be referred to as the "strong hand" or "pencil hand." The non-dominant hand can be referred to as the "weak hand," "helping hand," or "other hand."

AGOGO BELLS

Hold with high bell on top. Using a drumstick, play slightly away from the edge of each bell.

BASS DRUM

Strike the concert bass drum (not drum set bass drum) just off center with a big bass drum mallet.

BONGOS

The high drum is the lead drum; many traditional bongo patterns start with both hands working on the small drum. Whether sitting or standing, position the smaller head opposite the strong hand. Right-handed players put the smaller, higher-pitched drum on the left. By tilting the drums away from the body, the fingertips will fall into the proper playing position with fingers on the edge. One to two inches of the index and/or middle fingers are used. For elementary/middle school students, fingertip playing will suffice to get a good, clean open-tone sound.

CABASA

Cabasa can be used for shaker parts. Open the weak hand, palm up. Lay the beads of the cabasa on the palm. Make light contact with the fingers. Grip handle with strong hand and turn back and forth. For sixteenth notes, hold cabasa vertically and rub beads against the palm of the weak hand.

CLAVES

"Make your helping hand into a hot dog bun. Lay one clave lightly on top of the bun (alongside your thumb) like a hot dog, but leave room underneath for the mustard and coleslaw." This is one way to help children understand how to set up a resonating chamber with their hand. Strike the clave in the middle with the other clave. The sound should pop out.

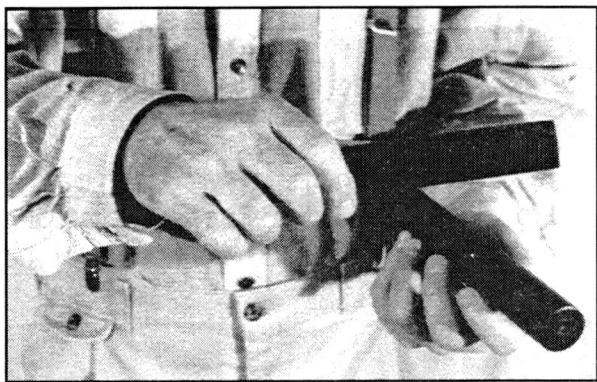

CONGA

High, medium, and low congas (Quinto, Conga, and Tumbadora) will simply be referred to throughout this book as high, med, or low when more than one pitch is required.

Basic conga tones include Tone (Open tone), Bass, Closed, Heel-Toe Closed, Open Slap, Closed Slap, and Slide. For ease of playing, the pieces in this book use only Tone and Bass.

T = Tone (also referred to as "Open tone") The drum should ring out with a full sound. Hit rim of drum with top edge of the palm. The hand should be flat and relaxed. This can be done with either hand.

B = Bass A powerful low-pitched accent. Drive the palm into center of the drum. The bass can be played by either hand.

APPENDIX

- When using congas, note that by changing the location of Basses and Tones, the entire feel of a rhythm can change. For example, the rhythm ♩ ♩ ♫ ♩ could be played in the following ways:

The changes in feel are remarkable!

- Also note with congas that accents are usually indicated as Basses, but the Tone can also be an accent. An example of this is the Conga rhythm.

COWBELL

Open your weak hand, palm up. Lay the cowbell on the palm with the mouth facing out. For a muted sound, leave the cowbell in contact with the hand. For a louder sound, hold away from palm with fingertips. Use a drumstick or a dowel to play across the mouth (wide end) or on the heel (narrow end) of the bell. M = Mouth and H = Heel.

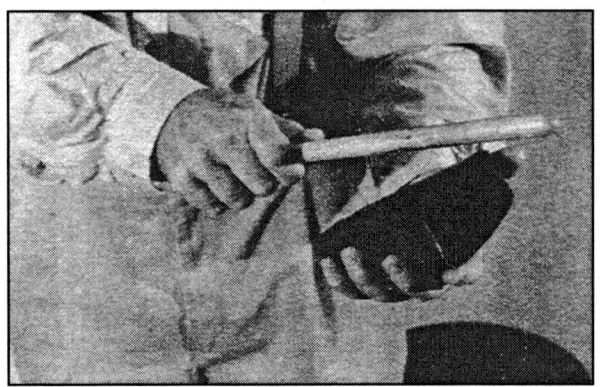
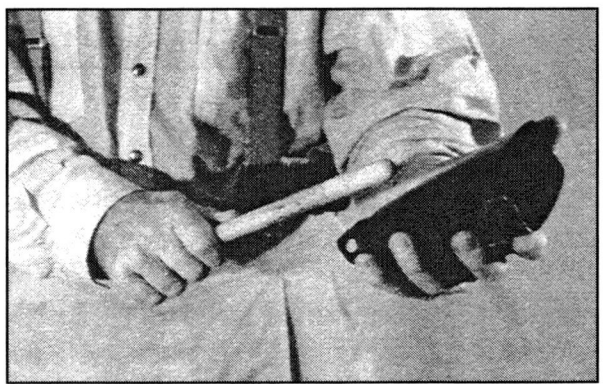

USE OF COWBELL

The cowbell is an instrument of critical importance. The sound cuts through the ensemble and can be heard by all. It can be played by the teacher or group leader to help keep the group together both in the teaching of the ensembles and in the actual performance.

If you are using the cowbell to direct the ensemble, the students can play sticks when practicing the regular cowbell part.

Changing to a more complex bell pattern toward the end of an ensemble will lift everything to a new level of intensity.

CYMBAL

Strike the edge (outer few inches) with a mallet or a stick.

GUIRO

Hold the head away from you with the tail toward your body. Place thumb and index (or middle) finger in the two holes. Use the strong hand to hold the thicker part of the scraping stick. Adults should scrape both down and up; children may find it easier to only scrape down with some patterns. They can substitute taps on the head of the guiro for the short scrapes in some rhythms.

For the ensembles in this book, play the guiro with a thin metal triangle beater to achieve more volume.

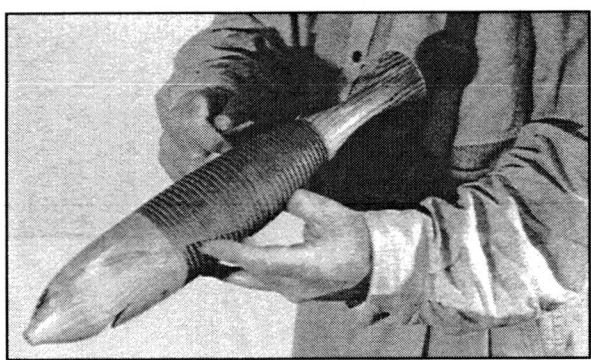

HAND DRUM

In this book, the term "hand drum" does not refer to congas and bongos, but rather to a member of the large family of frame drums. These hand drums have shallow shells and come in various sizes with diameters ranging from 10" to 22" in diameter. They are simply referred to throughout this publication as hand drums because that is the common name for them among elementary music educators.

The open tone is the only tone needed for the arrangements in this book. One approach to playing open tones on this drum is to hold the instrument vertically. Hold by the rim with the weak hand at the 12 o'clock location and strike with the middle or index finger of the strong hand a few inches from the edge of the drum, also at the 12 o'clock position.

In arrangements in this book, hand drum with mallet is indicated so that the drum will be loud enough to be heard while all of the other instruments are being played. Strike off center with the mallet.

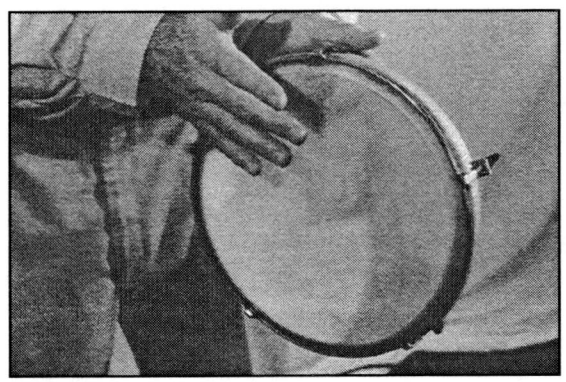

APPENDIX

MARACAS

For a precise clicking sound, grasp maracas near the ball, stiffen wrists, and move them with a small motion. For speed, lay two maraca handles across each other (like an X) and hold with one hand, shoulder high. Shake back and forth quickly with a small motion. This technique gives greater volume.

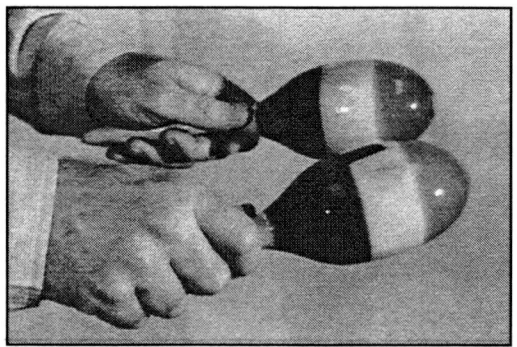 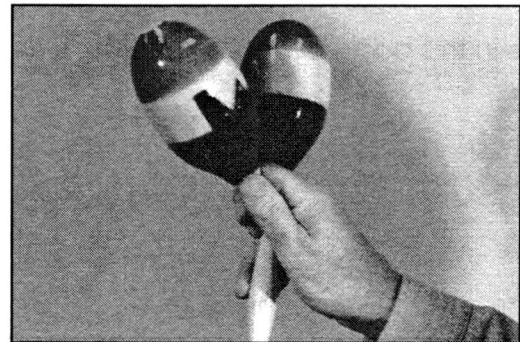

RATCHET

Turn the lever.

SHAKER

Hold parallel to the ground. Hold the shaker with the thumb closer to the body and the fingers on the side of shaker away from the body. The shaking motion is "forth and back," away from and back toward the body. Slower accompaniments require larger movements. As the accompaniment becomes faster, the movement needed is smaller.

VIBRASLAP

Place palm around the outside part of the handle and allow fingers to slide up into the curve of the handle. Hold with ball up. Slap the ball and it will vibrate, thus "vibraslap." Hold it level and it will vibrate longer.

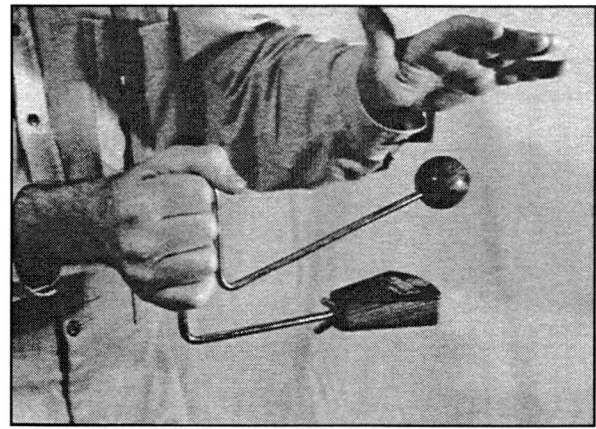

WHIP (SLAPSTICK)

For precise playing, hold it with the helping hand horizontally with the swinging section on top, and pick up the edge of the swinging section with the pencil hand. Throw it down while still holding the instruments horizontally.

For fun playing, hold it with your pencil hand and swing it as you would swing a paddle.

JIM SOLOMON

Author and clinician, Jim Solomon currently teaches music K-5 at Osceola Elementary School in St. Augustine, Florida, where he also works with a chorus, a recorder group, and a special percussion group for fifth grade students called D.R.U.M.

He teaches the Level I Orff Schulwerk Teacher Training Course at The Eastman School of Music in Rochester, New York. He is an MENC Nationally Certified Music Educator and was recognized as the St. John's County Teacher of the Year in 1991. He is a past Region IV Representative for the American Orff Schulwerk Association.

Jim received his Master Class Orff training from Memphis State University, Curriculum Course training from Hamline, Level II Kodaly training from Converse College, and an M.A.T. in Music Education from Jacksonville University. He has presented at nine previous AOSA National Music Conferences.

He has authored five books, the most recent of which are CONGA TOWN: Percussion Ensembles for Upper Elementary and Middle School (BMR08002), ©1995 Alfred Music Publishing Co., Inc.; and THE TROPICAL RECORDER, © 1997 Memphis Musicraft. Jim has also produced the video, CONGAS, BONGOS & OTHER PERCUSSION: A Guide to Technique.